WALKING *with* JESUS

Devotions for Autumn & Thanksgiving 2025

Editors of *Mornings with Jesus*
A GUIDEPOSTS DEVOTIONAL

A Gift from Guideposts

Thank you for your purchase! We want to express our gratitude for your support with a special gift just for you.

Dive into *Spirit Lifters*, a complimentary e-book that will fortify your faith, offering solace during challenging moments. Its 31 carefully selected scripture verses will soothe and uplift your soul.

Please use the QR code or go to **guideposts.org/spiritlifters** to download.

Walking with Jesus: Devotions for Autumn & Thanksgiving 2025
Editors of Guideposts

Published by Guideposts
100 Reserve Road, Suite E200
Danbury, CT 06810
Guideposts.org

Copyright © 2025 by Guideposts. All rights reserved.

This book, or parts thereof, may not be reproduced, stored in a retrieval system, or transmitted in any form or by any means, electronic, mechanical, photocopying, recording, or otherwise, without the written permission of the publisher.

Cover and interior design by Pamela Walker, W Design Studio
Cover photo by Dreamstime
Typeset by Aptara, Inc.

ISBN 978-1-961442-71-9 (softcover)
ISBN 978-1-961442-72-6 (epub)

Printed and bound in the United States of America
10 9 8 7 6 5 4 3 2 1

WALKING
with
JESUS

"Gratitude unlocks the fullness of life. It turns what we have into enough, and more. It turns denial into acceptance, chaos to order, confusion to clarity. It can turn a meal into a feast, a house into a home, a stranger into a friend…. Gratitude makes sense of our past, brings peace for today, and creates a vision for tomorrow."

—MELODY BEATTIE

O God of Creation, you have blessed us
    with the changing of the seasons.

As we welcome the autumn months,
    may the earlier setting of the sun
    remind us to take time to rest.

May the brilliant colors of the leaves remind
    us of the wonder of your creation.

May the steam of our breath in the cool air
    remind us that it is you who give us
    the breath of life.

May the harvest from the fields remind us
    of the abundance we have been given
    and bounty we are to share with others.

May the dying of summer's spirit remind
    us of your great promise that death is
    temporary and life is eternal.

We praise you for your goodness
    forever and ever. Amen.

"Autumn Months," by Author Unknown

Introduction

This is the day which the Lord hath made;
we will rejoice and be glad in it.

—Psalm 118:24 (KJV)

There are so many reasons to rejoice at the coming of autumn. As we settle into the waning days of the year, surrounded by the bounty of the preceding months, it's a natural time to shift our focus. The ever-shortening daylight encourages us to step back from our busyness and think about God's vast, generous universe. The Lord has taught us that, mirroring the salvation that awaits us after this life, the leaves that fall to the earth will return in the coming year. We are right to thank the Lord for all the goodness He bestows upon us, His cherished children. This includes not just our milestone events but the small blessings that uplift us: a crisp apple, the kaleidoscopic colors of a fall forest, walks with a loved one through the frosty air.

For millennia, fall has been the time when people have traditionally offered up thanks for the fruits of the year. From its earliest days, the United States uniquely embraced that spirit of thanksgiving: the precedent was well established after the iconic Pilgrim meal and periodic proclamations during the Revolution and early days of the American republic. Following a key Civil War victory, President Abraham Lincoln in 1863 proclaimed that the last Thursday of November would be a national day of Thanksgiving. Decades later, President Franklin Delano Roosevelt revived the tradition, proclaiming Thanksgiving to be an official United States holiday in 1942. As another wartime leader, he recognized that a nation enmeshed in a global conflict needed the spiritual sustenance that gratitude brings.

Our Bible shows us a richer, more ancient history of giving thanks to the God who both sustains and protects us. The Old Testament's Nehemiah 12:46 (NIV) referenced the days of David and Asaph, when "there had been directors for the musicians and for the songs of praise and thanksgiving to God." Those days under King David were good ones for the Israelites; there had been peace and unity. But other books recall God's intercession for His embattled people. Reflecting on their escape from the "hand of the foe" during the flight from Egypt, the Psalmist wrote, "Save us, LORD our God, and gather us from the nations, that we may give thanks to your holy name and glory in your praise" (Psalm 106:47, NIV).

Similarly, the writers of the New Testament looked on God as a benevolent and loyal protector, who'd redeemed His people through the sacrifice of His Son on the Cross: "Thanks be to God! He gives us the victory through our Lord Jesus Christ" (1 Corinthians 15:57, NIV). The Bible tells us that God not only expects our thanks but that our relationship with Him is built through our thanksgiving.

On a personal level, we can observe how gratitude for our everyday blessings fills us up in a way that only a loving Creator could provide. As Guideposts' own Dr. Norman Vincent Peale came to realize, "The more you practice the art of thankfulness, the more you have to be thankful for."

Thanksgiving becomes a powerful force for cultivating even more of God's goodness in our lives, whether in our relationship with Him or in our own hearts. Autumn offers us the perfect opportunity to cast our net wide and see the evidence of the Lord's mercy and affection all around us: a tree decked in beautiful foliage, a peaceful sunrise, the calls of migrating geese. And importantly, God gave us, as He did for Adam, the company of others, with whom we gather to share our thanks. As Elie Wiesel once wrote, "I feel gratitude in my heart each time I can meet someone and look at his or her smile." All of these blessings begin with our Redeemer.

The devotions in this book, written by beloved *Mornings with Jesus* authors, each present a unique, insightful perspective on the season and its themes. With a devotion for each of the days from October 1 through November 30, *Walking with Jesus: Devotions for Autumn & Thanksgiving 2025* is intended to help you enjoy this time and guide your steps during this special cycle of God's creation. Autumn offers a beautiful opportunity to renew your connection with the Lord who brings us so much. Over the next two months, we hope this book will help you strengthen your bond with God as you take His hand in love, gratitude, and prayer, and embrace the journey ahead.

Dear Lord, give us the discernment to see Your blessings in and around us—"as numerous as the stars in the sky" (1 Chronicles 27:23, NIV).

Now, our God, we give you thanks, and praise your glorious name.
—1 Chronicles 29:13 (NIV)

Lisa Guernsey

OCTOBER

WEDNESDAY
OCTOBER 1

*The heavens declare the glory of God;
the skies proclaim the work of his hands.*

PSALM 19:1 (NIV)

I SIT ON MY FRONT PORCH, which is adorned with pumpkins and dried corncobs, and watch the late afternoon soften to dusk. My old wooden rocker creaks a slow, satisfying rhythm, a metronome to the music of another day's passing. This quiet time spent alone with Jesus fills me with serenity. I reach for the steamy mug at my side, and heat emanates through the ceramic, warming my fingers and palms. When I raise the cup, my eyeglass lenses steam, and for a moment my vision is clouded, forcing me to focus on what I cannot see. I breathe in the scents of cinnamon and apples, true symbols of the season. I smell the earthy aroma of our maple's fallen leaves, and as I sip the cider, I'm reminded of the sweetness of autumn. I smile. Sitting here in creation, I feel the presence of the Creator.

As my vision clears, I see gold, red, brown, and orange leaves dance on the breeze. Moment by moment, almost too slowly for me to catch its subtle nuances, the sky transforms. The radiance of a vibrant sunset fills the heavens, and I gaze, transfixed by this masterpiece. I consider the bold shades Jesus selected to paint this season, perfectly mirroring the glorious hues of His eternal flame. I realize He's given me a picture—a self-portrait of sorts—where power meets peace, passion meets calm, and everlasting beauty is captured in an instant. I am in awe.

HEIDI GAUL

FAITH STEP

Take a seat outdoors, or near a window, during sunset. As you admire the bold masterpiece Jesus created, feel His presence and thank Him for His beautiful world.

THURSDAY
OCTOBER 2

Wait on the LORD; be of good courage, and He shall strengthen your heart; wait, I say, on the LORD!

PSALM 27:14 (NKJV)

BEFORE I MARRIED A FOOTBALL coach, I had no idea the game was such a science. In the early days of our marriage, when it was just us, I learned this by watching recordings with him, breaking it down play by play, and taking note of what each player did in order to strategize. Little did I know this skill would serve me well one day as the mom of a quarterback. Now most of the time, though not all, I have at least a clue what's going on when a certain play is called.

One of the most interesting things about football, I think, is the waiting. When both teams are on the scrimmage line, they're waiting for my son, Harper, to give the snap count. If someone can't wait and jumps offside, that person's team gets a penalty. So Harper acts sneakily sometimes and tries to make them jump by using a different cadence for the snap count. It takes intense concentration for the teams to wait for the perfect timing. Sometimes a penalty makes the difference between winning and losing the game.

Unfortunately, the culture we live in discourages waiting. Fast food, video on demand, overnight shipping—these have become our way of life. Yet the Bible seems to suggest it's in the waiting that we reap the best. Often that's when Jesus comes to us. And as He will come in clouds of glory when He returns.

GWEN FORD FAULKENBERRY

FAITH STEP

Instead of pining for the thing you want, set your heart today to look for Jesus as you wait.

FRIDAY
OCTOBER 3

Give thanks in all circumstances; for this is God's will for you in Christ Jesus.

1 THESSALONIANS 5:18 (NIV)

ONE MORNING RECENTLY WE NOTICED a puddle of water on the guest bathroom floor. And no one had used the shower. *Uh-oh.*

We grabbed towels, blotting the dampness to protect the nearby carpet. We finally located a leak somewhere around the base of the toilet. A few minutes later, we heard a gurgling sound from the shower as water bubbled up like an underground spring. Not good. Then I remembered another incident a year or two earlier when the plumbing backed up through our master bathtub. Surely not! I raced to the other bathroom, and you can guess what I found. An inch of anything but spring-looking water. *Yuck!*

The leakage eventually drained, and the problem didn't require an expert this time. For that we were extremely grateful. However, the mess left behind did necessitate a thorough cleaning of both tubs, one of which I had neglected for some time. I wasn't too pleased about the interruption in an otherwise productive day, as I completed the procrastinated job of scouring weeks of scummy buildup.

Later I felt Jesus's gentle nudge when I looked at the shiny surface of my clean tub. I actually heard myself uttering a prayer: "Thank You, Jesus, for that unwelcome interruption. It forced me to do an unpleasant task I had avoided far too long."

Giving thanks in everything is never easy. Some circumstances test us severely. That incident hardly mattered when compared to crises like illness, betrayal, unemployment, or a loved one's death. But the principle is the same.

Sometimes we need a heavenly prod to exercise gratitude, even to give thanks for a leaky toilet.

REBECCA BARLOW JORDAN

FAITH STEP

If you've never done so, begin a gratitude journal. Write down a recent circumstance for which you can give thanks. And every day, add something new—even if it seems unpleasant at the time.

SATURDAY
OCTOBER 4

This is why he can completely save those who are approaching God through him, because he always lives to speak with God for them.

HEBREWS 7:25 (CEB)

I'VE DRIFTED AWAY FROM A ministry I'm now determined to reinstate: Mug-of-the-Day.

My day starts with coffee but soon moves to tea. A self-confessed mug snob, I consider the vessel for the beverage almost as important as the drink. Significant size. Interesting shape. Ability to keep the beverage hot. And the mug must, must, must have a handle that fits four fingers comfortably. The grip is key.

My collection of pottery mugs includes souvenirs from vacations and speaking event locations, mugs with messages—*Hope Always, Write Anyway, A Mom Is . . ., Inspire*—and gifts from friends. I bought a look-alike mug for a friend of mine so we'd each think of the other while drinking our tea.

For a season, I used whatever mug I'd chosen as a prayer reminder that day. If the mug was a gift from a friend, I'd pray for that friend throughout the day. If the mug sported a camp logo, I prayed for the camp's ministry and staff. My Hope Always mug reminded me to pray for those struggling to keep their hold on hope. Even a souvenir mug could remind me to pray for those who live in that area.

I regret having let up on that practice. It's been too long since I looked at my tea mug as more than a container for a beverage. Jesus would never neglect an idea like Mug-of-the-Day. The Bible tells us He "ever lives to make intercession" for us. *Lives* for it! Unceasingly praying for His children. Constantly talking to God the Father about us and our needs.

The thought fills me with awe. He needs no reminders. He doesn't have a prayer list. He has a heart that remembers.

CYNTHIA RUCHTI

FAITH STEP

Our humanity makes us susceptible to forgetting. Consider your own Mug-of-the-Day reminders to pray for the people, topics, and ministries that matter to you . . . and to Him.

SUNDAY
OCTOBER 5

"I am the true grapevine, and my Father is the gardener. He cuts off every branch of mine that doesn't produce fruit, and he prunes the branches that do bear fruit so they will produce even more."

JOHN 15:1–2 (NLT)

TEN YEARS AGO, MY MOM planted a rosebush in our backyard. Each spring its old-fashioned roses overtake the side of the gardening shed. They are light yellow, edged in apricot and crimson. The blooms are fragrant and as big as my hand. The bush itself towers over the top of the eight-foot shed. I love everything about it. But it didn't get that way on its own. My mom shared the secret of pruning with me.

Every autumn when the last bloom drops to the ground, I go to town with the pruning shears. I deadhead all the old blooms. I trim off shriveled branches. And then I pare the bush way back. It looks pretty sad after I trim it up. Shorn. Spindly. Empty.

Pruning isn't my favorite gardening practice. I don't love getting pricked by thorns or hacking away at tough branches, but I know if I let it go, then new growth can't take place. I actually stunt its potential if I don't cut off the dead portions.

Jesus feels the same way about our lives. He wants to trim out all the old growth. He is persistent when it comes to trimming the "dead" areas of our lives. The diseased parts of our souls, the unhealthy thinking, the areas of our lives that are limiting us? Those have to go. He wants to unleash the potential for growth in our lives. He wants to do a new work in our hearts and our minds. And I think we should let Him.

SUSANNA FOTH AUGHTMON

FAITH STEP

Take a walk outside and study the plants and trees. Growth is what Jesus is all about. Ask Him what areas He would like to prune out of your life.

MONDAY
OCTOBER 6

And he said: "Truly I tell you, unless you change and become like little children, you will never enter the kingdom of heaven. Therefore, whoever takes the lowly position of this child is the greatest in the kingdom of heaven."

MATTHEW 18:3–4 (NIV)

By early September, my nine-year-old granddaughter's thoughts had already turned to trick-or-treating. "Well," Lacey announced one day, "I guess I could always be a princess for Halloween. But that seems so childish."

Her three-year-old brother looked at her earnestly. "So what?" he asked with a puzzled expression. "You *are* a child."

Jesus used a child as an example of the Christian faith and what makes a person great in heaven's eyes. We may think we have to become a great theologian or accomplish great works to impress Him, but what Jesus values most is a humble, childlike spirit. We can only come to Him through our vulnerability and need, with no agenda of our own, trusting

Him to work in our life. Once we realize our utter dependence on Jesus, then we can receive His greatest blessings.

Sometimes I get weary of trying to figure out things I'll never understand. I can knock myself out attempting to fix myself, other people, and every problem I see around me. That's when I need a reminder of the attitude that demonstrates genuine faith.

When her little brother pointed out the obvious, Lacey's response was, "Thanks a lot, buddy. You really lightened me up." How often my burdens would be lightened if I let go of my striving and unrealistic expectations, and if I simply remembered my identity. I am a dearly loved child who can always trust Jesus to take care of me.

DIANNE NEAL MATTHEWS

FAITH STEP

In what ways are you growing in your childlike faith? What burdens would be lifted if you could develop that quality more? Ask Jesus to help you fully depend on Him and receive His blessings as a child.

TUESDAY
OCTOBER 7

*Let us not become weary in doing good,
for at the proper time we will reap a harvest
if we do not give up.*

GALATIANS 6:9 (NIV)

MY HUSBAND, JEFF, AND I had been working in the yard all day, and it was too late to start supper, so we decided to pick up burgers at a drive-through. When it was time to pay, the worker told us, "No charge. The people in front of you paid for your meal." What a lovely surprise! To pay it forward, we picked up the check of the person behind us in line. I craned my neck to get a look at the lucky soul who'd benefited from our kindness. Would she wave, throw a kiss, honk? Disappointingly, she didn't acknowledge our gift.

Why hadn't I expended such effort to see the person who'd *bought* our meal? Easy. Rather than wanting to *offer* gratitude, I expected to *receive* it. It's fortunate that Jesus didn't expect gratitude for all the good He did. The blind, the lame, and the lepers appreciated His healing, but most of them were too excited to hang around and thank Him. Individuals in the crowds who may have been touched and awed by Jesus's words didn't thank Him, although many were changed forever. How often do I remember to thank Jesus for His ultimate sacrifice so that I can enjoy eternal life?

If I expect gratitude for the good I do, then I'm sure to be disappointed. It's never a good idea to keep score. Jesus didn't. Doing good and loving others should be its own reward.

PAT BUTLER DYSON

FAITH STEP

Ask Jesus to remind you not to expect gratitude for your good deeds. If He is pleased with you, that is thanks enough.

WEDNESDAY
OCTOBER 8

"Enter through the narrow gate. For wide is the gate and broad is the road that leads to destruction, and many enter through it. But small is the gate and narrow the road that leads to life, and only a few find it."

MATTHEW 7:13–14 (NIV)

A FEW YEARS AGO, MY HUSBAND and I hiked a remote area of the Ottawa National Forest. We've done a lot of hiking, including sections of the Superior Hiking Trail, so we felt fairly confident. But the old-growth forests provided a new experience. Instead of clear paths cutting through thick underbrush, we found stretches of huge trees in all directions, with smooth forest floor coated with a bed of fallen leaves. No dirt path visible. Nothing to indicate which way to go, except for small trail markers nailed to trees.

At first, we could scan into the distance and spot the next marker and know which way to head. But sometimes trail markers were missing. We found several broken off or resting in the dirt near the base of a tree.

When the trail seemed to disappear, I forged ahead. Eventually I pulled to a stop. "I have no idea where I'm going."

My husband muttered playfully, "That never stops you." We backtracked to the last marker and tried a new direction until we found the elusive next symbol.

Our hike that day reminded me of the adventure of following Christ. He might give me a glimpse of the final destination, but for most of my life journey, I'm aiming just for the next small trail marker up ahead. My steps lead through rocky terrain, beautiful vistas, and swampy bogs. Often God's guidance is as clear as the white diamond markers on tree trunks, giving me courage for tough climbs and wet slogs. Other times, I struggle to see the path. I flounder in a likely direction for a while and then need to backtrack a bit, stand still, and listen until Jesus gets me back on track. His narrow path is the only one that will lead me safely through the wild forests of my life and home to my eternal destiny.

SHARON HINCK

FAITH STEP

Ask Jesus to show you clear trail markers for the next step in your journey on His path.

THURSDAY
OCTOBER 9

*Because of the L*ORD*'s great love we are not consumed, for his compassions never fail. They are new every morning; great is your faithfulness.*

LAMENTATIONS 3:22–23 (NIV)

Last night I crawled into bed and snuggled down under my comforter. I lay awake for a long time even though I was exhausted.

Sometimes I have a hard time falling asleep. My mind races with the events of the day. I replay conversations and what I would or should have said if my brain were quicker than it is. I think about my boys and my interactions with them. I think about issues in our family and the problem-solving that I do with my husband, Scott.

It is no small miracle when my thoughts finally fade into oblivion and I can actually drift off to sleep. The mind is curious that way. It is always working, planning, rethinking, and sometimes regretting.

But there is one absolutely lovely thing about falling asleep. I get to wake up to a new day. New chances. New choices. New opportunities. And according to the Scriptures, new compassions. *New compassions.* What a truly hope-giving thought.

Because of Jesus's faithfulness, His love is inexhaustible. It doesn't run out or run dry. Jesus's character never changes. He is love. When the sun cracks the sky, I get to awaken to a new day full of His constant and consistent compassions.

I am thankful for a good night's sleep. But mostly I am thankful for new mornings full of Jesus.

SUSANNA FOTH AUGHTMON

FAITH STEP

Find a chalkboard or whiteboard. Write down the things that you have been regretting lately. Take an eraser and wipe them clean. With Jesus we have a new day full of His compassion.

FRIDAY
OCTOBER 10

"And the seed that fell on good soil represents those who hear and accept God's word and produce a harvest of thirty, sixty, or even a hundred times as much as had been planted!"

MARK 4:20 (NLT)

So often, reading this parable or hearing it taught as I grew up in the church, the focus was on the harvest. This verse is rightfully linked with Jesus's words in John 4:35, which says the fields are ripe for harvest.

In the church I grew up in, this harvest, ripe for the picking, has to do with winning converts to the faith. Since it came after Jesus's conversation with the Samaritan woman and the subsequent conversion of many in her town, that makes sense. But so often we think, *What do I have to do to get busy harvesting?* Yet Jesus is not saying the good seed represents a farmer who does the harvesting. It represents the soil. Good soil, in which seeds can grow.

And how does soil become good? As a gardener, I can tell you: the soil can't become good on its own. In fact, the gardener has to work with it. It has to be broken apart so that is softened. It has to have rocks and weeds pulled from it. Good soil has organic matter in it: nutrients produced by the decay of dead leaves or manure. Circumstances in my life that, at the time, felt like "manure" have often been used by God to help me to grow.

So if Jesus is telling us to be "good soil" so that our hearts can be fertile ground for His Word, perhaps we will have to submit to Him, allowing Him to break us, to pull the weeds of materialism and worry, and perhaps even "fertilize" us with what feels like dying to self.

KERI WYATT KENT

FAITH STEP

How is Jesus trying to work the soil of your heart? Are you resisting Him because it feels difficult? Ask Him to help you see the purpose of the struggles in your life.

SATURDAY
OCTOBER 11

*Devote yourselves to prayer,
being watchful and thankful.*

COLOSSIANS 4:2 (NIV)

GIVING THANKS IS SOMETHING I incorporate into every prayer in two specific ways. First, I thank Jesus for what He's done for me in the past, and then I thank Him for what I trust He'll do in the future.

Recalling prayers that He's already answered bolsters my faith to believe He will do it again. This practice gave me courage to trust Jesus when my husband and I began the process of buying and moving aboard a sailboat. I thanked Jesus for providing suitable housing for our family every time He'd moved us to a new location in the past. I thanked Him that His timing for our moves had always proven perfect and that He'd gone before us to prepare a place for us in the hearts of our new neighbors. Focusing on His faithfulness and wisdom that oversaw our past relocations brought courage to trust Him for the next.

Then I expressed gratitude in advance for what I trusted Jesus would do. I thanked Him for providing the finances necessary to buy the boat and a suitable place to moor it. I thanked Him for providing a vessel with every amenity necessary to serve His purposes. I thanked Him for helping my husband learn about the systems needed to keep the boat livable. Expressing gratitude for things yet to be seen or done grew my faith. It squelched uncertainties and birthed anticipation.

Prayer is more than making requests. It includes giving thanks. God's Word issues this command over and over again for my benefit. Making it a regular practice is helping me to have courage to trust Jesus in every situation.

GRACE FOX

FAITH STEP

Thank Jesus for a specific prayer He's answered in the past. Now thank Him in advance for caring for the details of a concern yet to be resolved.

SUNDAY
OCTOBER 12

For God alone my soul waits in silence;
from him comes my salvation.

PSALM 62:1 (ESV)

I HAVE ALWAYS LOVED SILENCE. I miss it a lot. Before we moved to the Upper Peninsula of Michigan, I drove to the Hiawatha Forest for one week every month. I left my flock of sheep and my work as a neonatal nurse practitioner to get away from the noise and to write.

I'd never known such quiet.

I heard the refrigerator cycling and my heartbeat in my ears while waiting for sleep. The cabin had no phone, no TV, no Internet—not even cell phone coverage. I wrote in silence and kept a list of things to research. A trip to town and five bucks in the donation jar at the Falling Rock Café got me online once a week. That was plenty.

I was relaxed, prayed up, and productive. When we moved north, we brought our share of human and electronic noise. Now I write in our tiny lake house, rich in quiet (except for loon calls).

Then, a few months back, I lost the hearing in my right ear. It turns out, for me, deafness does not equal silence. Like the phantom pain felt by an amputee, tinnitus—the brain's consolation prize for loss of aural input—clangs in my head.

I'm cranky. Disquieted. My friends and I are praying. My hearing is better, and I'm grateful. Still, the silence is gone.

But quiet may still have a chance. Jesus knew the value of pulling back from chaos. He withdrew often to talk with His Father. During a busy time, He encouraged the disciples to come away to a solitary place to rest. I can still keep silence before God as an act of worship—even if it doesn't sound the way it used to.

SUZANNE DAVENPORT TIETJEN

FAITH STEP

Silence can be holy—an act of worship. Sit in silence today. Try ten minutes or more. Imagine Jesus sitting there with you. He will be.

MONDAY
OCTOBER 13

He humbled you, causing you to hunger and then feeding you with manna, which neither you nor your ancestors had known, to teach you that man does not live on bread alone but on every word that comes from the mouth of the LORD.

DEUTERONOMY 8:3 (NIV)

I LOVE BREAD. I CAN HONESTLY say I'm passionate about it. I love crusty Italian bread with holes the size of the Grand Canyon. I love French bread with its soft, almost creamy center and crisp crust. I love the sturdy but soft Greek bread holding the marinated meat of a gyro. I love thin naan with its darkened bubbles across the surface.

I think God deliberately used bread in this passage as opposed to other things we eat—like vegetables or meat—because the Word of God is like bread. Nourishing, comforting, filling. Just as bread can be varied, Scripture can hit me in different ways depending on where I am in my life.

God can test us with trials in our lives to show us that we need Him more, or so we find we need Him in a different way. We often see trials as ways the devil is torturing us, but Jesus tested His own disciples to determine if they were faithful. It wasn't just so He could know their faith but also so that the disciples could grow and mature in their faith.

When in trials, digging into the Bible is often the only way to stay sane. And while in those difficult stages of your life, the Word of God is like bread: it can be different each time you read it, but it's always filling. It's hard to thank God for our trials, but they can show us how to depend on Jesus more, just as we depend on bread to survive.

CAMY TANG

FAITH STEP

Are you struggling with something right now? Take the time to read more of God's Word, and find sustenance, comfort, and fulfillment there. Eat the bread of heaven and find a new way to cling to Jesus.

TUESDAY
OCTOBER 14

Trust in the LORD *with all your heart and
lean not on your own understanding;
in all your ways submit to him, and he will
make your paths straight.*

PROVERBS 3:5–6 (NIV)

DEPENDING ON THE SEASON, MY small town might be surrounded by acres of grass, sweet-smelling meadowfoam blossoms, or fields of corn. Lots of corn. I love driving the country roads, watching as the stalks grow taller week by week. During autumn, some farms use harvested stalks as mazes for the public to enjoy.

Walking a corn maze can be fun or daunting, depending on your perspective. It exhilarates me to enter one, utterly clueless of how I'll find my way out. Solving a problem through patience and logic, laughing over missteps or dead ends, makes for an entertaining afternoon.

Coursing through these agricultural puzzle paths, I glimpse similarities to real life, like days I fret, unable to see what lies ahead. Or the challenges I've encountered, and the periods I've felt as if I wasn't getting anywhere. The times I've made a wrong turn and found myself more than a bit lost. Even people and experiences that I've come to recognize as dead ends are represented among the stalks.

But unlike time spent inside a corn maze, with Jesus I'm never truly lost. Jesus is walking alongside me through life's tough twists and turns. I can depend on Him to help me solve mysteries and direct my footsteps all the days of my life. And when my days on earth are done, I know the path I'll take will lead me straight to Him.

HEIDI GAUL

FAITH STEP

Think about a situation in which you feel confused or stuck. Meditate on Proverbs 3:5–6 and pray for Jesus's guidance until you see a way out.

WEDNESDAY
OCTOBER 15

Give praise to the LORD, proclaim his name; make known among the nations what he has done. Sing to him, sing praise to him; tell of all his wonderful acts. . . . Remember the wonders he has done, his miracles, and the judgments he pronounced.

1 CHRONICLES 16:8–9, 12 (NIV)

LAST NIGHT, WE GOT TOGETHER with our good friends the Couches. My husband, Scott, and I have known Shane and Marty since college. We couldn't help remembering our early days of friendship. Those were formative days of growth and joy. In college, Shane and I became friends performing in lip-sync battles together. We took our fun seriously. Scott and Shane took a statistics class together off-campus. Their struggle with high math established their friendship. Marty and I got to know each other after she and Shane got married. We had our kids during the same season, and our third babies were born only days apart. While launching their counseling ministry, Shane and Marty attended our church plant. It was a huge encouragement for us to have them there. As our kids grew, we celebrated and had parties with dancing and board games. Through the years, we have also supported each other through surgeries, emotional struggles, and career moves.

Remembering is a way we honor our friendship. In our relationship with Jesus, looking back can help us move forward. Remembering all that He has done for us builds our faith. By naming those moments when Jesus intervened on our behalf and set our feet on a path of healing, we cement our bond with Him. He loves us. There is no reason to doubt Him. Look at all He has done for us.

SUSANNA FOTH AUGHTMON

FAITH STEP

Remember all that Jesus has done for you. Make a timeline of the moments that He has come through for you, and thank Him for each one.

THURSDAY
OCTOBER 16

"When someone has been given much, much will be required in return; and when someone has been entrusted with much, even more will be required."

LUKE 12:48 (NLT)

I'M NOT SURE THEY'LL HAVE a bathtub."
My kids and I were shopping the dollar section to fill boxes for overseas children in need. One of them came across some tub toys, which prompted my response. The toys revealed the gap between an existence in a developing country and ours.

Wow, what a small part of this globe I live on, I thought.

I've seen extreme poverty in Honduras and Mexico. Whenever I've witnessed how the other nine-tenths live, I'm drawn to ask God why.

Why, Lord, do I have so much and they so little? What am I doing with my much to multiply their little? I am no millionaire, and I work hard for sure. But there's nothing about me that makes me entitled to more than someone else. They work hard too.

We give of our resources to help others, and I think that's all good and necessary. But my spirit says there's more truth to uncover.

When I look deeper into my heart, I wonder whether my lifestyle reflects my greatest riches—that is, the abundant forever I look forward to because of Jesus. How invested am I in sharing that wealth, the only kind that never loses its value and ensures eternal payoffs? Am I thriving from dividends of joy, peace, love, gratitude, *Christlikeness*, and hope? Am I committed to giving away this wealth?

Anyone can enjoy the riches of Jesus's saving grace. Those of us who've already received that abundance need to take seriously His command in Luke 12:48. Giving doesn't refer exclusively to material wealth. The joy and hope and love of Jesus's abundance that is ours for the taking is meant to be given away with abandon. There's no limit to His riches, if only we'll take fully to heart the reality of how rich we are in Him.

ERIN KEELEY MARSHALL

FAITH STEP

Are you enjoying your spiritual wealth?
Find a way to share it today.

FRIDAY
OCTOBER 17

This hope is a strong and trustworthy anchor for our souls. It leads us through the curtain into God's inner sanctuary.

HEBREWS 6:19 (NLT)

I'D ALWAYS PICTURED AN ANCHOR as something a fisherman might toss over the side of his boat when he wanted to stay in one spot. Then I visited a lighthouse memorial in Oregon and met a real anchor, up close and personal. It was in the traditional shape that's so familiar, often used as a symbol or as a jewelry design. But it was huge! I couldn't begin to guess how many tons it weighed, or how many sailors it would take to manage the anchor and its chain. But I felt sure that this anchor would not have a problem in keeping a ship from drifting.

I love how the writer of Hebrews used the anchor, a popular symbol in the early church, as a metaphor for the hope we have in Jesus Christ. Life can sometimes resemble a stormy sea, with unexpected circumstances and raging emotions tossing us about. We wonder if our life will turn into a shipwreck. Even when life seems like smooth sailing, we may be in danger of drifting from the truth, blissfully unaware of the world's pull on us. During all of life's stages, we need to be anchored in Jesus. Our hope in Him is the only way to find stability for our life and security and peace for our soul.

No matter what troubles or heartaches this earthly life brings, I have the promise that Jesus is with me every step of the way. He will never stop loving me and will provide everything I need. One day He will welcome me to a perfect home, where we'll live for all eternity. Surely that hope is enough to keep me from being tossed about or drifting off-course.

DIANNE NEAL MATTHEWS

FAITH STEP

The next time you face stormy seas, lay hold of your anchor in Jesus. Remind yourself of what it means to hope in Him.

SATURDAY
OCTOBER 18

For I resolved to know nothing while I was with you except Jesus Christ and him crucified.

1 CORINTHIANS 2:2 (NIV)

Each time I read this verse, I gulp. Can I really aspire to this sort of single-minded focus? Can I learn to value Christ so much that everything else becomes like nothing by comparison?

When we were newlyweds, my husband and I went on a backpacking trip in the Grand Teton Mountains with a youth group. As we prepared, we learned about priorities. When you have to carry everything on your own back for miles of hiking in high elevations, you get wiser at deciding what matters most. I've heard that some experienced backpackers will even cut off the handle of their toothbrush to reduce the weight of their pack by another fraction of an ounce.

Before we left, I looked around our apartment. I liked our microwave, our books, our piano. I enjoyed a dresser full of clothes and a curling iron on the bathroom counter. But for our adventure in the mountains, all I really needed were the basics of survival. Ten days lugging a tent, sleeping bag, and food taught me a lot about how much is nonessential.

Sometimes in our walk of following Christ, we get bogged down by the nonessentials. There are plenty of interests, activities, or ambitions that feel important. They aren't necessarily bad things. But they sometimes threaten to crowd out the central purpose of life. When we're serious about following Christ through the difficult climbs of discipleship, we want to pare down to what matters most: knowing Him and His crucifixion.

SHARON HINCK

FAITH STEP

Think about the backpack of your spiritual life. Are there any nonessential things weighing you down?

SUNDAY
OCTOBER 19

And he said, "The kingdom of God is as if a man should scatter seed on the ground. He sleeps and rises night and day, and the seed sprouts and grows; he knows not how."

MARK 4:26–27 (ESV)

JESUS TEACHES THAT YOU AND I are like farmers. One of our roles is to sow seeds. Most often we do it without even realizing it. For instance, a mother sows seeds by caring for her home and for little people as she goes about her normal routines. Those seeds take root and sprout and grow in the lives of her kids. I see evidence of this in my granddaughters' lives when they cradle and dress their dolls in the same manner that their mother cares for their younger siblings.

A pastor or parent sows seeds of love for God's Word. My mother sowed these into my life when she sat at the kitchen table and prepared her lessons for the women's Bible study she attended.

Folks who clean up after the church potluck sow seeds of servanthood. Those who give thanks even when it's hard sow seeds of gratitude. Those who sit at the bedside of a dying loved one sow seeds of compassion.

We don't consciously think about our actions as sowing seeds, but Jesus says that's what they are. He says those seeds take root in other people's lives. They sprout, they grow, and eventually they produce a harvest (Mark 4:29). We really have no idea when or how this all takes place. It just does. It's a spiritual mystery in which our actions and attitudes play a part in other people's lives, so let's sow seeds that result in a harvest of righteousness.

GRACE FOX

FAITH STEP

Take one intentional action to sow seeds of joy in someone's life today.

MONDAY
OCTOBER 20

I praise you, for I am fearfully and wonderfully made. Wonderful are your works; my soul knows it very well.

PSALM 139:14 (ESV)

MY DAUGHTER AND I SHARE a love of handmade pottery. At a high-quality art fair, we'll head for the pottery booths every time.

One of her husband's most romantic gifts to her was a kiln he found at a garage sale. Now that's love.

The footed pitcher-like pottery bowl I use to make pancake batter is a little off. Its handle droops like a left arm after a stroke. The rim isn't what one would use as a standard for something "level." The glaze is uneven in one spot. But I love that footed bowl because a friend made it. Its supposed flaws are what make it unique, one of a kind. It was made and given with heart.

The amateur potter apologized for how misshapen it is, compared to the perfect picture in his mind.

But its charm is in its imperfection.

Why do we have such a hard time adopting that attitude toward ourselves and others? Jesus still holds the world record as the only perfect human to have lived, and even He was noted as not being particularly attractive on the outside. Isaiah says it wasn't His appearance that drew people, but the Spirit of God within Him. "He had no form or majesty that we should look at him, and no beauty that we should desire him" (Isaiah 53:2, ESV).

We were handcrafted for Him and by Him. His workmanship. Even with our droopy handles, He thinks we're charming.

CYNTHIA RUCHTI

FAITH STEP

They say every woman has an instant answer to the question, "What one thing would you change about your looks?" Is today the day to start seeing that feature through the eyes of one who appreciates the unique?

TUESDAY
OCTOBER 21

The Lord is my shepherd, I lack nothing. He makes me lie down in green pastures, he leads me beside quiet waters, he refreshes my soul. He guides me along the right paths for his name's sake.

PSALM 23:1–3 (NIV)

WHEN SCHOOL STARTS UP AGAIN after any break, I go through several days of chasing my tail. After I drop the kids off, I'm eager to tackle the to-dos that I've put off while my young ones are home.

However, a curious thing happens as I walk through my door. My brain freezes and I lose all ability to prioritize. I stare at my list feeling useless about where to begin.

This phenomenon doesn't throw me as much as it used to. I've learned to sit down and pray first, asking Jesus to focus me on His action plan.

Ernest Hemingway is credited with saying, "Never mistake motion for action." Based on how Jesus lived, I think He'd advise us to sit still more often than not, instead of scurrying around wasting time. This advice can seem backward to our motion-driven culture; someone who looks busy must be accomplishing a lot, right?

Read carefully today's verses from Psalm 23, and notice what the Lord does first for the writer, King David. After David acknowledges that he lacks nothing (including the ability to accomplish his God-given tasks), he writes that the Lord makes him lie down in green pastures. Rest is the first task the Shepherd gives David. After that, the Shepherd gently nudges him to action, leading him first by quiet waters to refresh his soul. Once David is refreshed, Jesus knows he's ready to be guided along the right path for the day.

Never feel as if you're wasting time by pausing to listen for Jesus to speak to you. In fact, prioritize that over the to-do list. You'll be much better prepared for what the day throws at you.

ERIN KEELEY MARSHALL

FAITH STEP

Read Luke 5:16 to remind yourself that Jesus paused with His Father in order to refill for the coming demands.

WEDNESDAY
OCTOBER 22

Because of the Lord's great love we are not consumed, for his compassions never fail. They are new every morning; great is your faithfulness.

LAMENTATIONS 3:22–23 (NIV)

I WAS HIKING WITH A FRIEND who had recently survived a battle with breast cancer. She had chosen to have a mastectomy. About the same time, doctors discovered abnormal cells in her uterus, so she also needed a hysterectomy. The recovery from both surgeries was brutal.

"I'm so thankful all that is behind you," I said.

She paused, and with a heaviness in her voice she said, "Me too. Last year was rough and I was hoping this year would be better, but . . ." she choked back tears and told me about her adult son's health issues that involved multiple trips to urgent care and eventually a diagnosis of a lifelong autoimmune disease.

She continued to talk about how hard life is sometimes. She'd had hard things happen, one after another, and it felt like more than she could handle. I had no words of comfort. As I listened, I silently prayed, *Please, Jesus, give her a break.* When she paused, I asked her, "How are you doing? How are you making it through each day?"

"Every morning I watch the sunrise. The sky turns beautiful colors as the sun peeks over the horizon. It's God's way of faithfully greeting me, and this puts a little joy in my heart to start the day," she said.

I had prayed for her to have a break, but God was already doing that. Every morning at daybreak, He reminded her of His great love, compassion, and faithfulness with each sunrise that she enjoyed.

JEANNIE BLACKMER

FAITH STEP

What is an action you can take today, such as watching the sunrise, to remember Jesus's great love for you?

THURSDAY
OCTOBER 23

And my God will meet all your needs according to the riches of his glory in Christ Jesus.

PHILIPPIANS 4:19 (NIV)

FLIPPING THROUGH THE PAGES OF a photo album, I smile. An old picture depicting my husband, tiny daughter, and me at a farm's harvest fest caught my eye. A massive red barn dominates the background, but the main focus is an overfull wheelbarrow holding a giant pumpkin. At well over 100 pounds, it fairly screams for attention. Back then, I suppose that was my goal. I wanted the biggest, best, and brightest of everything, even pumpkins.

Time passed, and changes occurred in our household. As Christina grew, harvest and Halloween decor seemed to shrink in importance. Huge pumpkins were replaced by just a few ordinary ones. And after she moved out and married, I scaled back to displaying only a few small ones on my porch.

But during those years, a more important difference took place within our family. We found Jesus.

Through Him we discovered that life's greatest treasures aren't necessarily flashy or big or beautiful. They don't require exorbitant price tags. Instead, these jewels overflow with simple goodness and wholesome pleasure—a bowl of butternut squash soup on a brisk evening, a leaf-peeping drive through a hardwood forest, a long hug from a loved one.

But the most valuable prize I claim is the relationship I share with Jesus. Through Him, I've found riches I'd never imagined. Far superior to the largest pumpkin and more hearty than a cup of butternut squash soup. Because my every need and desire has been satisfied within His limitless glory.

HEIDI GAUL

FAITH STEP

List some of autumn's simple pleasures, and the ways they remind you to celebrate the glory of Jesus.

FRIDAY
OCTOBER 24

And now, dear brothers and sisters, one final thing. Fix your thoughts on what is true, and honorable, and right, and pure, and lovely, and admirable. Think about things that are excellent and worthy of praise.

PHILIPPIANS 4:8 (NLT)

I AM A GREAT FAN OF letting things slide. Laundry. Dishes. Doctors' appointments. Flu shots. Washing the car. Washing the children. They don't seem to mind.

But sometimes this approach doesn't yield the results I long for. Like life with an empty kitchen sink and children that smell like roses.

But I think that letting things slide can be a great life strategy. I think I need to be strategic about what I let slide. Like wondering what people are thinking about me and focusing on the negative. Those things can slide. Irritability? Anger? Nagging? Whining? Worrying? Slide. And the things I can't afford to let slide? Laughing. Walking with my friends. Noticing the turning colors of the leaves. Finding more recipes with dark chocolate. Kissing my boys. Dating Scott. Loving Jesus. These are the things I should never let slide. These are the wonderful things of life that I want to focus on. I want to focus on the beauty of life and let the things slide that suck the joy out of my day.

Jesus has given us the great gift of life. He has given us these days to live out. We don't really get to choose what our days look like. But we can choose the lens we use to look at them. We can choose to focus on the beauty and goodness of our days and let the rest slide . . . or we can focus on the ugly things in life and get bogged down in the muck of negativity.

SUSANNA FOTH AUGHTMON

FAITH STEP

Join me in letting things slide . . . and choose to see today through the lens of beauty. Tell Jesus all the things in your life that bring you joy and fill you with peace.

SATURDAY
OCTOBER 25

On the day I called to you, you answered me. You made me strong and brave.

PSALM 138:3 (NCV)

As an amateur green thumb, I'm reading about tough plants for tough places. Plants are like people. Some are happier in warmer climates. Some can go longer than others without a drink of water.

Some thrive in sunlight; whereas others sunburn easily, requiring shade. And some enjoy a robust four-season climate, gladly withstanding snow and freezing temperatures.

Tough plants can endure adverse garden conditions, such as drought, shade, heavy clay soil, or dry rocky soil. Likewise, tough people can endure adversity and hardship yet persevere and still thrive. Spiritually, I want to be like a "tough plant for tough places"—able to endure adversity and still bloom and thrive—despite tough situations in life.

But I'll need help. God, the master gardener, creates both plants and people, giving each unique attributes and characteristics. Deep-rooted spiritual strength, stability, security, and resilience come from Jesus—from abiding in Him by staying planted in His Word.

Psalm 138:3 confirms that Jesus will make me strong and brave if I call out to Him. So, rather than wonder if I'm the right type of "toughness," I'm asking Jesus to make me spiritually tough—so I can survive and thrive—despite whatever adverse conditions I may face in the garden of life.

CASSANDRA TIERSMA

FAITH STEP

Spiritually, are you a tender annual, hardy perennial, or a tough person for a tough place? As a reminder that it's Jesus who gives strength and courage, visit a local plant nursery to find a tough plant for a tough place (i.e., a plant that's drought tolerant, not fussy about soil type) for your home or garden. Ask Jesus to make you strong and brave for the tough situations in life.

SUNDAY
OCTOBER 26

Don't worry about anything; instead, pray about everything. Tell God what you need, and thank him for all he has done.

PHILIPPIANS 4:6 (NLT)

As a young Bible study teacher, I often asked the question, "What prayers has God answered for you lately?" The absence of current, "meaty" answers bothered me. I wanted to hear more than the "Jesus-gave-me-a-parking-spot" kind of prayer from my students. In the sometimes awkward silence, one or two would regularly share their survival of a near accident or serious illness earlier in their lives.

As I matured, however—and quit judging—I soon realized a class member's answer (or silence) didn't always indicate the neglect of a vital prayer life. It could simply reflect a quiet personality, the inexperience of a new believer, or even the need for more time to reflect before responding.

Recently I asked myself that same question. No current, "meaty" answers emerged. Well, age and fading memory do go together, don't they? All of us experience times when answers to prayers don't slip off our tongues readily, and we fall back on "old" testimonies.

Maybe you pray fervently and specifically. But children, carpools, and overcrowded schedules take their toll. Paul's reminder—"thank him for all that he has done"—gets squished between piles of laundry. By the time Jesus answers your prayer, you've forgotten the request—or that He answered it.

Maybe that's why I've started thanking Jesus *before* He answers—for those answers. As He knows our needs (and requests) even before we ask (Matthew 6:8), isn't He trustworthy enough to thank for His responses—even before we receive them?

We can trust God for His answers, whatever they are. And if asked, we can offer fresh testimonies—because we've already expressed gratitude ahead of time.

REBECCA BARLOW JORDAN

FAITH STEP

Keep your prayer requests in a small notebook. Thank Jesus for His answers as soon as you pray them. And review that notebook weekly.

MONDAY
OCTOBER 27

*Yet he commanded the skies above
and opened the doors of heaven.*

PSALM 78:23 (ESV)

MY KIDS LOVE TO SWING. Actually, I do too. Something about the fresh breeze—feeling as if I could launch and soar into the air, unencumbered by gravity—thrills my heart.

I think a swing can draw a person closer to Jesus. That seems simplistic, I understand. But some of the best, most affecting truths come from unassuming sources, such as a piece of playground equipment most of us have enjoyed at one time or another.

Much as a swing pushes my heart to aim high, so does God's Word. Focusing on Jesus's promises of a future with Him helps me envision my real life that hasn't even begun yet: my someday life in heaven with my Savior.

Could it be that He wants my heart to soar with Him even now, buoyed with only the hope of the joys to come? Yes, I'm sure of it.

The reason Jesus's followers are still on earth is to bring Him glory by shining His light in this world. When we aim high for Him, He can take us to greater heights than we could imagine.

The more we trust Him to take us beyond our finite scope, the greater the possibilities. This concept isn't just a pie-in-the-sky fairy tale; we are created to aim for more than what we can reach on our own. Every day the Lord wants to carry us higher, if only we set our sights on His realm, a whole world beyond this one.

ERIN KEELEY MARSHALL

FAITH STEP

How big is Jesus's power in your life? Ask Him to help you aim for more of Him, and expect Him to amaze you with new views of Himself.

TUESDAY
OCTOBER 28

*"But ask the animals, and they will teach you, or the birds in the sky, and they will tell you; or speak to the earth, and it will teach you, or let the fish in the sea inform you. Which of all these does not know that the hand of the L*ORD *has done this?"*

—JOB 12:7–9 (NIV)

How had the day gotten away from me? It was almost dusk, and I hadn't exercised. With darkness encroaching, it was too risky to ride my bicycle, so I'd walk. I grabbed my headphones and set out, anxious to catch up on the news of the day as I exercised. About the time I reached the end of the block, my phone died. How would I occupy my mind? The silence was deafening.

I hustled along the empty street, preoccupied with worries. My route took me to a wooded area of the subdivision that hadn't been developed. As I rounded the bend, a slight movement caught my eye, and I stopped. A doe and two fawns grazed in the clearing not twenty yards away. The sight took my breath away. I stood watching for several minutes before the deer bounded away. *Jesus, was that You? How I needed You to tell me to slow down, to appreciate the beauty around me!*

I remembered a sonnet by nineteenth-century poet William Wordsworth, "The World Is Too Much with Us." Guilty as charged. How long had it been since I'd looked at the clouds, sniffed a flower, or paused to listen to a bird's song? On my way home, I slowed to a stroll and talked to Jesus. As always, He showed me the way.

PAT BUTLER DYSON

FAITH STEP

Go for a nature walk. Take a bag with you to collect leaves, feathers, and rocks. When you get home, look at all the items and thank Jesus for nature's bounty.

WEDNESDAY
OCTOBER 29

But we Christians have no veil over our faces; we can be mirrors that brightly reflect the glory of the Lord. And as the Spirit of the Lord works within us, we become more and more like him.

2 CORINTHIANS 3:18 (TLB)

A FRIEND'S KITCHEN AND LIVING ROOM are being remodeled. What a job! Workers have removed cupboards and doors. They've ripped out flooring, walls, and windows. Eventually they'll install new cabinets, countertops, carpet, French doors, and light fixtures.

This process hasn't been easy for my friend's family. They disposed of their old appliances, placed their belongings in storage, and moved into a rental for five months. A hassle? Yes, but worth it because the makeover will result in a more comfortable home.

Sometimes the Holy Spirit performs a makeover on us. He surveys our attitudes and behaviors and says, "Hmmm.

That pride's gotta go. So must the grumbling and the gossip." Then He sets to work.

Slowly, He strips the characteristics that grieve Him and then builds new qualities into our lives. Qualities such as love, joy, peace, patience, and kindness—the familiar ones listed in Galatians 5.

Sometimes the makeover feels painful, embarrassing, or downright annoying. But the Spirit is the pro. He knows what He's doing, and it's smarter to let Him work than to argue.

Letting the Holy Spirit work in us as He wishes results in greater Christlikeness, and we'll reflect His beauty to those around us.

GRACE FOX

FAITH STEP

Be honest. What attitude needs a makeover—impatience? Pride? Envy? Invite the Lord to strip away any attitude He finds offensive and replace it with one that honors Him.

THURSDAY
OCTOBER 30

"If anyone is thirsty, he should come to Me and drink! The one who believes in Me, as the Scripture has said, will have streams of living water flow from deep within him."

JOHN 7:37–38 (HCSB)

I ONCE HEARD A SPEAKER FROM the Cherokee Nation explain his belief system, which he said was more of a philosophy than a religion. He said his mother raised him with a concept called "going to water," which he still practices every day.

"When you go to water, you basically cleanse your face and hands with water, and as you do this you think of something of value that you can contribute to the world that day."

He went on to talk about the "white path," which he said comes from the idea that you choose the path you take through the day. He chooses the white path—which means he chooses to have a good effect in someone's life that day.

I'm trying to teach my kids to "go to water" too. The girls about have it down, but Harper has yet to see the purpose of washing your face. Perhaps if I tell him Cherokee warriors do it, the concept will become more appealing.

I love the idea that as we wash our faces in the morning, we are thinking of something valuable we might bring to the world that day. I also think it's biblical to acknowledge that we choose what path to take.

The beauty of both of these things for the Christian is that Jesus is the water. We draw from the source of Living Water and offer Him to the world. We can take His hand and know He walks with us, guiding our feet down the right path and helping us do good in the lives of others every day.

GWEN FORD FAULKENBERRY

FAITH STEP

As you wash your face this morning, ask the Lord to show you someone who is thirsty today, that you may offer them a drink of Jesus.

FRIDAY
OCTOBER 31

There is no fear in love. But perfect love drives out fear, because fear has to do with punishment. The one who fears is not made perfect in love.

1 JOHN 4:18 (NIV)

MY BOYS LOVE TO SCARE me. The other night, I was walking into my room when Addison, my thirteen-year-old, jumped out from behind the door and yelled, "Boo!" I screamed and lurched to the side, my hands immediately closing into fists. Addie jumped back, knowing my response would be to strike at whatever had just scared me. He couldn't stop laughing. I was irritated and said, "What in the world?" Addie laughed and said, "Mom, you look so funny when you are scared." I wasn't laughing. My heart was racing. I was scared, ready to fight.

I tend to collect fears: fear of spiders, fear of heights, fear of giant children jumping out from behind doors. But fear wasn't a part of Jesus's original plan. There is no reason for fear when you are surrounded by perfect love. The moment Adam and Eve stepped out of that love to shape their own destiny—fear rushed in. Hence, we all have that heart-pounding response toward anything beyond our control or understanding. Fear sucks the joy out of life.

Jesus said, "I have come that they may have life, and have it to the full" (John 10:10, NIV). It is hard to live life to the full when we are freaking out. Jesus came into this world to forgive our sins, to restore us, and to help us share His love with others. When we invite Jesus to shape our destiny, He begins to cast out every fear, surrounding us with His perfect love—joy in its fullest form.

SUSANNA FOTH AUGHTMON

FAITH STEP

What are you afraid of? Tell Jesus about it.
Believe that you are shielded by His perfect love.
Step out today and live unafraid.

NOVEMBER

SATURDAY
NOVEMBER 1

"But small is the gate and narrow the road that leads to life, and only a few find it."

MATTHEW 7:14 (NIV)

A LONG, NARROW ROAD RUNS THROUGH my town. It's a mountain railway that carries eighteen trains a day. Living in a historic railroad town is nostalgic, with the lonesome call of train whistles, clanging bells, and the high-pitched sound of steel wheels squealing on the rails. (Even as I write this, I'm enjoying the sound of train whistles calling in the distance.) I especially love gospel train songs that compare railroads to the road to heaven—songs about getting on trains bound for glory.

Narrow paths—railroad tracks, in my case—have featured repeatedly in my life. As a child living next door to a track, I'd hear the train going by during the night. When I had small children of my own, we took a camping trip in the Pacific Northwest. Heavy rain forced us out of our tent and into a motel in town. It wasn't until the middle of the night that we realized a train trestle was right behind that old two-story motel—making for a very loud, clattering stay. Eventually, I took my children on summer vacations at a small log cabin by a lake, where, on the railroad track behind it, a train would rumble by early every morning.

Now my children are grown, and they sometimes ride the train to visit me here in the small town I call home. Though they can find their way here, today I'm praying that they'll all find the narrow road that leads to life through faith in Jesus Christ.

CASSANDRA TIERSMA

FAITH STEP

Are you praying for loved ones to find the narrow road that leads to eternal life through Christ? Ask Jesus to show them the Way.

SUNDAY
NOVEMBER 2

Let your light so shine before men, that they may see your good works, and glorify your Father which is in heaven.

MATTHEW 5:16 (KJV)

THE WIND TORE LEAVES, LIMBS, and power lines. The storm raised rivers and felled giant maples. Winds toppled so many power poles that it will be days before power, phone service, and the Internet are restored.

Because we live far from the nearest town, we have a generator we can run for short stretches to keep food in the freezer from spoiling. But the generator can't handle normal electrical usage, so we've limited ourselves to necessary electrical draws.

It's natural to assume that with the power out, we would catch up on reading. There's a reason pioneers' and pilgrims' eyes went bad reading by candle glow. We've propped flashlights so their circle beams land on the page we're reading.

But as frugal as we are to save the hardworking generator, I caught myself looking at the lamp on my desk and, reminiscent of a Dickens character, internally asking, "Please, sir, could I have this one small light?"

If you're like me, you often feel that your influence to make a difference for others is no more influential than one small light in an otherwise pitch-black world. Little difference? Switch it off for a moment, and you'll realize that its influence is much more significant than you imagine. People crave something that will help illuminate the mess they're in and send the darkness fleeing. Jesus is that Light. We serve as His reflections. Jesus is asking, "Could I have your one small light?" It does make a difference.

CYNTHIA RUCHTI

FAITH STEP

Let your light shine brightly today, and before the day's end, make sure someone who needs hope sees it in and hears it from you.

MONDAY
NOVEMBER 3

Through Jesus, therefore, let us continually offer to God a sacrifice of praise—the fruit of lips that openly profess his name. And do not forget to do good and to share with others, for with such sacrifices God is pleased.

HEBREWS 13:15–16 (NIV)

WHEN MY SPIRITS ARE LOW, spending time praising Jesus is a sure way to allow His peace and joy to fill me again. It can feel like a sacrifice—an effort that costs something—to form words that focus on His greatness when I'd rather remind Him of everything wrong. I'm grateful that He invites us to be real with Him, to pour out our hurts and concerns. However, I also know that it's important to spend time professing His name and acknowledging the truth.

The other day I was stuck in bed dealing with a lot of pain and weakness. I tried to offer praise but couldn't focus long enough to string thoughts together. "Lord, thank You for creating the world and . . ." My mind wandered away from any specifics. "Jesus, You are so loving and . . ." I'd shift my position and lose the last part of the sentence. I wanted so much to praise Him with my whole heart and soul and mind, but I floundered.

Then I remembered the alphabet game. On long car trips, we'd look around for objects starting with the letter A, then when we'd run out of ideas, we'd move on to B. I wondered if I could use that same tool to help me praise. "Lord, I'm so grateful for the flavor of apples. Thank You for creating them. For my friend Amy. For the authority You have over this world. For authors whose books have nourished me. You designed butterflies and beaches, and You are bountiful and full of blessings." As I worked my way through the alphabet, my heart grew more peaceful and I drifted off to sleep.

SHARON HINCK

FAITH STEP

Praise Jesus for His qualities and His gifts, using the alphabet tool.

TUESDAY
NOVEMBER 4

May your unfailing love be my comfort, according to your promise to your servant.

PSALM 119:76 (NIV)

We heard the freeze warning on the news, signaling an early winter.

My beloved gardens were still producing in early November: seven-foot-tall pepper plants and tomato vines nestling multiple clusters of green tomatoes. Most of the perennials would simply fall asleep like bears in hibernation, returning the following spring.

But what about my twenty-five potted annuals, including my green and flourishing ferns? Before nightfall, my husband and I gathered the plants, covering them with sheets on the back porch. They looked like lumpy ghosts.

The next morning I checked the damage. Most of the perennials survived, but the beautiful, trailing sweet potato vines lay shriveled, yellow, and brown, along with my colorful coleus plants. Too sad. The annuals would die.

Just when the winter doldrums were descending, I walked into the living room and found my husband had started a blazing fire, comforting and warm. Not only that, he'd collected a sack full of green tomatoes. That night we enjoyed a Deep South staple—fried green tomatoes—for the first time.

Most of us dislike winter, endless days of unchanging, frigid weather, threatening to shrivel our faith and discourage our spirits. Like those dying plants, we may feel useless and void of color.

Jesus taught me a lesson that day, one I often forget. Every season has a purpose. Jesus is like that warm, blazing fire, beckoning us to sit awhile and partake of His comfort and warmth. Even in the harshest circumstances, He will cover us with His love and may even surprise us with good things that emerge from that season, if we'll watch for them.

REBECCA BARLOW JORDAN

FAITH STEP

Think about a time when it felt like winter in your life. What good things came out of those experiences? Today thank Jesus for His continuous covering of love.

WEDNESDAY NOVEMBER 5

Come away, my beloved, and be like a gazelle or like a young stag on the spice-laden mountains.

SONG OF SONGS 8:14 (NIV)

THIS LAST WEEKEND I WAS away speaking at a women's retreat in Washington with my friend Melissa.

We did a lot of laughing. Mostly, Melissa laughed at me because I could not maneuver climbing in and out of a top bunk bed. (Why are the rungs so far apart? Why are sleeping bags so slippery? Why do I not have any upper arm strength?)

We had chats long into the night. It was a moment to get away from life and refocus, relax, and regroup.

I like the word *retreat*. In my mind, I hear it as a full battle cry. "Sweet mercy, run for your lives! *Retreat!*" I picture myself, arms flailing, running all out, breathing hard to get to a place of peace. A place where the clamor of life eases up enough so I can hear myself think and give Jesus a chance to connect with me.

I am not an army tactician, but I have watched enough Civil War movies to know that when the guy in charge yells, "Retreat!" it is so those who are fighting the battle can back up and get together with him. They need to disengage, get out of the fray—and they need to do it at a full-out run, so he can give them a new course of action.

I don't think a retreat has to be at a camp . . . though it is nice when it is. But I do think anytime you change your surroundings it helps you refocus. So this morning, after I take the kids to school, I am going for a walk at the park near my kids' school. So I can get together with Jesus and find out what's next. I want Him to call the shots. Retreat.

SUSANNA FOTH AUGHTMON

FAITH STEP

Find a place of peace where you can sit and listen to Jesus. Tell Him that you want Him to call the shots in your life today.

THURSDAY
NOVEMBER 6

But one thing I do: Forgetting what is behind and straining toward what is ahead, I press on toward the goal to win the prize for which God has called me heavenward in Christ Jesus.

PHILIPPIANS 3:13–14 (NIV)

MOVING OUT OF A HOUSE we'd lived in for twenty-three years proved to be a real eye-opener. I couldn't believe all the unnecessary stuff we'd accumulated in closets, cabinets, drawers, and the garage. We saved the worst for last: the attic. Crawling over the patches of flooring, I discovered items I thought we'd gotten rid of long ago. We made several trips to donate items at Goodwill and drove away from a huge pile for the garbage collectors to pick up. *Never again*, I vowed.

Yet three years later I found myself once again preparing to move. Although nothing like the previous experience, I was still surprised by how much I had to purge from our belongings. But hanging on to old papers, unused makeup, and home decor that doesn't fit anymore isn't my worst problem. I also have a hard time letting go of past mistakes, hurts, and disappointments. Whenever I talk about what "should have been" or "could have been," my daughter says, "You gotta let it go, Mom. Just let it go."

Dwelling on negative aspects of the past paralyzes me. It keeps me from growing into the person Jesus wants me to be and prevents me from being a blessing to others. It's important to review our failures to see what lessons we can learn. But once we've been forgiven and restored, it's time to put the guilt and shame behind us and press on toward what Jesus has in store for us. It's time to "just let it go."

DIANNE NEAL MATTHEWS

FAITH STEP

What "old stuff" do you need to purge from your life so you'll be free to move forward and live the life Jesus intends for you? Jot down your list, pray over it, then destroy it.

FRIDAY
NOVEMBER 7

Be careful that you do not forget the LORD, who brought you out of Egypt, out of the land of slavery.

DEUTERONOMY 6:12 (NIV)

I HAVE AN EARLY 1900S SINGER treadle sewing machine table sitting in my foyer. I have fond memories of learning to sew with my Granny Bowers on that sewing machine. I inherited the treasured piece when she passed on to her reward, and I think of her often when I see it in our home.

There are other things that remind me of Granny. The smell of cold cream, because she kept a big pink jar of Pond's cold cream in her vanity. The sight of yellow roses, particularly growing in a large bush, because Granny loved the huge yellow rosebush that framed one side of her house. An old-fashioned single-seat swing tied to a large tree with rope, because Granny often pushed me on a swing like that.

It doesn't take a lot for me to be reminded of Granny because I associate her presence with so many things. Likewise, I associate Christ's presence in my life with little reminders as well. A song on the Christian radio station. A cross on a necklace. The sight of a rising or setting sun. So many reminders to keep me aware of my Lord. Like those reminders of my granny, the reminders of Christ give me peace and comfort, letting me know that He is everywhere.

RENEE ANDREWS

FAITH STEP

Find three things today that remind you of your Lord.

SATURDAY
NOVEMBER 8

*"Do not grieve, for the joy of the
L*ORD *is your strength."*

NEHEMIAH 8:10 (NIV)

A FRIEND FROM HIGH SCHOOL SENT an unexpected email. My delight quickly turned to sadness. Her daughter, not yet forty, was battling an aggressive breast cancer and faced another critical round of treatments. My friend was asking for prayer, hoping to widen the circle of the many who were already praying.

What could have been the saddest email in my inbox that day turned a corner when I checked out my friend's daughter's blog. The young woman had been keeping a public gratitude journal during her journey. The posts were cleverly written, even on the worst of days. They celebrated life in all of its messiness and pain, all its hidden joys and unexpected humor. She'd invited each of her siblings and her parents to post to commemorate her final chemo treatment before surgery. And she wouldn't take "No," "I can't," or "That's too hard" for an answer. She knew "too hard" well. And writing a blog post wasn't it.

But the assignment would have challenged any of us. She asked her family members to write a blog post titled "What's So Good about Cancer?" They each discovered something profound they could say. I read the series of posts as if unearthing treasures of love and respect these family members shared and their resilience in the face of a formidable enemy. Overarching all was joy irrespective of the young woman's circumstance. It was the kind of joy only Jesus can give.

That's one of the marvels of following Him. The joy He provides isn't a reflection of circumstances. Many times, it is completely, utterly contrary to our circumstances. A joy people notice. I did.

CYNTHIA RUCHTI

FAITH STEP

Consider the most trying difficulty you're facing right now. Dare to ask, "What's so good about it?" Find a buried nugget of gratitude.

SUNDAY
NOVEMBER 9

*The light shines in the darkness, and
the darkness has not overcome it.*

JOHN 1:5 (NIV)

THIS TIME OF YEAR IN Oregon's Willamette Valley, evening arrives quickly, like a thick veil muting the colors and sounds of the day. As darkness falls, the crisp air chills further, a hint of winter's approaching cold. But for now, I'm swept up in the anticipation of spending an hour or two with loved ones around our backyard firepit.

I grab my heavy jacket and a blanket to join the others as they settle into lawn chairs. The glow of the flickering flames softens our features, and gentle laughter punctuates our hushed conversations. We reminisce and dream, sipping steamy mugs of cocoa and debating over how to roast the perfect marshmallow. Moments of silence still our thoughts, and we bask in the peace of these simple pleasures.

Joy fills the atmosphere. To me, the quiet marks the presence of Jesus. We are safe within this circle of light that pierces the darkness surrounding us. But a more powerful Light lives within us, brightening our spirits during challenging times, softening the sharp edges of our sometimes harsh world, and protecting us with the wisdom of His Word. From Him, through Him, and for Him, we are flames aglow with warmth and joy as we overcome the darkness.

HEIDI GAUL

FAITH STEP

How can you share the light of Jesus? Sit in front of a fireplace, light a candle, or gather around a firepit or chiminea, and pray for opportunities to share the Light with others.

MONDAY
NOVEMBER 10

"For who has understood the mind of the Lord so as to instruct him?" But we have the mind of Christ.

1 CORINTHIANS 2:16 (ESV)

My fingers stumble over the piano keys as I squint at the hymnal. The notes are a blur, and I can't make sense of them. Why am I hitting all the wrong notes? I rub my eyes. Of course. I forgot my glasses. I fetch them from the other room and am soon back to playing with renewed confidence and ease.

Anyone with vision problems knows the feeling when things don't look right. No matter how beautiful a painting is, if you can't bring it into focus, it's a confusing mass of colors. A book of poetry could have lyrical, transcendent lines, but those words can't stir your spirit if they are only gray squiggles. But with glasses or contacts, we can again see things the way they are meant to be seen.

I wish it were as simple to correct my spiritual focus. Much of my life, I seem to squint myopically at the world around me, unable to see the beauty in my cranky neighbor, the holy grace in another pile of laundry, and the precious opportunity in a work setback. When I look into a mirror, my vision problems are especially bad as I see only flaws and inadequacies obscuring the image of a beloved child of God.

I need to look through new eyes. Thankfully, God gives us that ability. We have the mind of Christ. We can view the world, others, and ourselves through a new perspective—one that brings God's grace into clear focus.

SHARON HINCK

FAITH STEP

Is there something in your life that doesn't look good to you? Ask God for the mind, the perspective, the vision of Christ, and then take another look. Can you see His beauty hidden in that situation?

TUESDAY
NOVEMBER 11

Pray without ceasing.

1 THESSALONIANS 5:17 (KJV)

My brother-in-law needed a place to stay. Our simple life in the country offered the kind of reflection time he craved while he waited for the sentence that would change his life dramatically for the next seven years.

So my husband and I took him in for two months and adapted to his habits, as he did to ours. We quickly became accustomed to his peanut M&M addiction.

When he left our house to begin serving his court-ordered sentence, we held on to the ever-present bowl of peanut M&M's and turned it from addiction to a prayer ministry. Guests and family who knew the story were told, "You're welcome to the M&M's, but if you take one, use it as a reminder to pray."

The grandkids were especially interested in a prayer ministry connected with a big bowl of M&M's. "Who are you praying for now, Josh?" I asked as he swiped another from the bowl.

"The whole world."

"Oh. OK." Can't fault a child for knowing the whole world needs prayer.

Five-year-old Andy grabbed a chocolate-covered peanut, bowed his head and leaned it against the buffet on which the bowl rested, ate the peanut, then promptly grabbed another and bowed his head again.

What had we started?

When I'd caught Josh with his hand in the bowl too many times one afternoon, I asked, "Now be honest with Grammie. Who were you praying for just now?"

"I was just telling Jesus how much I love Him."

"Um . . . carry on."

CYNTHIA RUCHTI

FAITH STEP

How many quick but deeply meaningful "Jesus, I love You so much!" prayers pepper your day and mine? I have to believe He's at least as pleased to hear it as I am to know my grandsons—whatever the motivation—are faithful to say it.

WEDNESDAY
NOVEMBER 12

*Many are the plans in a person's heart,
but it is the LORD's purpose that prevails.*

PROVERBS 19:21 (NIV)

It should have been a great Saturday afternoon of bowling. The youth group with which I volunteer was planning a major tournament of staff versus kids, and competition would be fierce. Trash talking abounded, and we adult staff members had our reputations to defend.

But that day turned out to be very rainy, and when we arrived at the bowling alley, not only was there a birthday party there, but other families had also come to bowl since the weather was bad. No lanes were available.

Instead, we recruited a few parents and some college students who'd shown up to be drivers, and everyone went to Nickel City, a video-game arcade. It ended up being a fun outing.

I admit I got kind of frazzled with the last-minute organizing, and I remembered ruefully how our plans are not always God's plans. I always thought the verse referred to "big plans," such as what career to go into or whether to buy a house. A foiled bowling trip seemed like something too trivial for God to want to bother Himself with, and something I could handle by myself.

But I think the point of the verse isn't about big plans or little plans. God wants us to realize that in life, there will always be change, and that He is the one in charge. And sometimes we have to relinquish our sense of control and be flexible.

Jesus talked about the rich fool who built barns for his abundance of grain, making plans to eat, drink, and be merry, but then died the next day. His plans took a major U-turn. His plans weren't God's plans.

CAMY TANG

FAITH STEP

Whether you're a planner or not, are you able to graciously accept changes in plans? Are you flexible? Pray for Jesus to help you relinquish control and practice flexibility.

THURSDAY
NOVEMBER 13

Ever since I first heard of your strong faith in the Lord Jesus and your love for God's people everywhere, I have not stopped thanking God for you. I pray for you constantly.

EPHESIANS 1:15–16 (NLT)

PAUL'S ATTITUDE OF GRATITUDE AMAZES me. Several times throughout his letters in the New Testament, he mentioned "remembering" others and giving thanks for them. The book of Ephesians is one of Paul's epistles that records his frequent habit. After spending two years in Ephesus previously, Paul wrote this book in prison, possibly under house arrest.

OK, maybe he did have more time to focus and remember in this more isolated setting. But knowing Paul, he still spent time not only writing but also sharing about Jesus to anyone who crossed his path.

Paul didn't thank Jesus once for the beloved friends and new believers he'd met, then forget about them. He never stopped. Obviously, he had ministered to them. But they also touched his life. And then Paul did more than just remember those people. He prayed constantly for them.

When Jesus spoke to Paul (then Saul) on the road to Damascus and blinded him temporarily, He changed the former persecutor's life—dramatically (Acts 9). That encounter not only resulted in a dynamic missionary preacher but started a spirit of gratitude forever in Paul's life.

After reviewing Paul's letter, I decided to top my new "thanksgiving" list with the names of people Jesus has brought into my life through the years: friends, family, church members, neighbors—whoever Jesus brings to mind.

Remembering so many may be challenging, and the list will keep growing. But if I can simply ask Jesus to help me maintain a grateful heart, and review that list of names often, that's a good start.

REBECCA BARLOW JORDAN

FAITH STEP

Make a list of people who have influenced your life. Then write notes to let them know how grateful you are, and that you are praying for them.

FRIDAY
NOVEMBER 14

The Lord is not slow in keeping his promise, as some understand slowness. Instead he is patient with you, not wanting anyone to perish, but everyone to come to repentance.

2 PETER 3:9 (NIV)

I LIVE IN THE NORTHWEST, WHERE heavy rains define autumn and winter. Every year, as the temperatures drop and the skies drip, I begin winterizing my garden. I follow the weather forecasts, watching for the final smattering of dry days. That's when I pick the last of my crop of tomatoes and line them up along my home's sunniest windowsills.

Then I wait. The sheer light filtering through the glass turns their green skins red. But it takes a lot of time and patience. Days, then weeks, can pass with no obvious change before the first few begin to show orange and red tints. Some seem to change color overnight, while others lag slowly behind. Deep into fall, most of the fruit has ripened, brightening our dinner plates.

Those tomatoes in the windowsill remind me of the different paths to Jesus. Some find Him early, as children. Others take longer, needing first to experience some of life's blessings and heartaches along the way. I was one of those late harvests.

Just as I don't know which of my tomatoes will ripen first or last, I also can't guess when some of my friends and loved ones will begin their transformation to become believers. My privilege is to watch, pray, and turn them toward the Light. He will take care of the rest.

HEIDI GAUL

FAITH STEP

Which of your friends can you bless today? Who can you help turn toward the Light? Make a list, and pray for each person's transformation according to God's perfect timing.

SATURDAY
NOVEMBER 15

"Come to me, all you who are weary and burdened, and I will give you rest."

MATTHEW 11:28 (NIV)

GRANDMA, I WANT TO SNUGGLE with you," said my three-year-old grandson, Luke. I hoisted the feverish tyke onto my lap, and he placed his head on my chest. There he dozed for the next hour. And there I sat, cuddling my precious cargo.

After months of constant go, go, go, I relished this hour as an unexpected gift. I felt sorry that Luke was ill, but rocking him provided guilt-free rest for my weary body and soul. For that, I felt thankful.

Psalm 23:2–3 (NIV) says the Lord's aware of our needs. "He makes me lie down in green pastures, he leads me beside quiet waters, he refreshes my soul." As a shepherd cares for his flock, so Jesus cares for us. He knows when we're weary, and He knows how to refresh us.

Sometimes He provides rest through an extended getaway or sabbatical. Other times He provides mini vacations—an overnight escape or a relaxed evening with a spouse or close friend. Most often, He sends soul-refreshing snippets—a cup of tea sipped on the back deck, a stroll around the block, or a few minutes to read undisturbed.

Are you weary today? Jesus knows. Acknowledge Him as your Shepherd, and ask Him for green pastures and quiet waters. Ask Him to refresh your soul.

GRACE FOX

FAITH STEP

Sometimes choices we make cause weariness. Ask yourself if this is true in your situation. Are you getting enough sleep? Can you delegate some of your work? Do you need to learn to say no to other people's requests for your time and energy?

SUNDAY NOVEMBER 16

Jesus replied, "Anyone who loves me will obey my teaching. My Father will love them, and we will come to them and make our home with them."

JOHN 14:23 (NIV)

*H*OME, SWEET HOME. Perhaps you grew up in a sweet home. Maybe you did not. Nonetheless, today's verse contains a concept of home that is perfect, and it's not a place I ever leave because Jesus never leaves me. He promises that if I love Him, I'll obey Him, and then He and the Father will come to me. They'll make Their Home in me wherever I am.

But what does this mean? I'm sure I can't conclusively capture it, but here are some things it means to me. It means a father who provides for me, a brother who's always in my corner, and a mother who gathers me in her arms like a hen with her chicks. It means safety, and security, and a place where I can hide. It means joy. It means I am known with all my warts—and loved anyway. It means forgiveness. It means

I'm fed. It's a place I can rest, a place to find comfort when I'm sad, and a place for celebrations when things go well.

The home that Jesus provides for me is where every day starts and every day ends. It's the comfort I take with me wherever I go that keeps me grounded. His home reminds me of who I am. Because Jesus makes His home in me, I'm accepted as well as challenged, and disciplined as well as tenderly loved.

GWEN FORD FAULKENBERRY

FAITH STEP

Draw a picture of what home looks like to you. Furnish it with all the things Jesus brings when He comes to make His home with you.

MONDAY
NOVEMBER 17

"Don't give holy things to dogs, and don't throw your pearls in front of pigs. They will stomp on the pearls, then turn around and attack you."

MATTHEW 7:6 (CEB)

ONE OF THE MOST IRREPLACEABLE, valuable things we possess is our time. We cannot go out and buy more time; we cannot go into the kitchen and whip up a couple of extra hours.

And yet time is one of the things we squander the most easily. We waste time, spending it doing things that sap our energy. If someone asked you to give them money, you might decline, but when they ask you for your time, how do you respond?

There's nothing wrong with giving someone your time, but I have often been sucked into commitments I should have avoided by thinking, *Well, it's only a few hours of my time.* I forget time is a pearl of great price.

This odd saying of Jesus forces us to consider: what are the holy things I possess? What are *my* pearls—the things I value most, the things that are rare and precious to me?

My stuff is not holy. My possessions are not my pearls. But the hours I have each day—these are precious. As my children get older and move toward independence, I realize I do not get these days to do over. When other people try to demand those pearls from me, sometimes the most holy thing I can do is refuse.

One of the more countercultural ways I spend time with my family is to take a weekly Sabbath. The Bible tells us the Sabbath is to be kept holy. Those precious hours, when I set aside my work and busyness to focus on my relationships with God and my family—they are pearls. In order to protect them, I sometimes have to say no to the requests of others. I think Jesus would approve.

KERI WYATT KENT

FAITH STEP

What do you need to say no to in order to protect the holy things in your life? Think particularly of your schedule—have you thrown your pearls before pigs?

TUESDAY
NOVEMBER 18

*My soul will find joy in the LORD and
be joyful about his salvation.*

PSALM 35:9 (GW)

MY FRIEND ASKED IF I had been living under a rock. She'd just mentioned binge-watching a television show with her teenage daughter. My response had been, "Who's Marie Kondo?" Later, a quick online search filled me in about the tidying expert known around the world through her best-selling books and popular show. In Marie's own words, her goal is to help people "transform their cluttered homes into spaces of serenity and inspiration." I felt encouraged by her short list of commonsense rules for keeping a house in order. Her approach recognizes the connection between our environment and our emotional condition. Marie urges her clients to evaluate whether to keep or discard an item by asking themselves if it sparks joy.

When you think about it, having a daily quiet time is a way to declutter the mind and keep it tidy. As I focus on

God's Word and prayer, His Spirit realigns my priorities. I confess any sins nagging at my conscience and receive forgiveness. I turn over any burdens weighing me down into Jesus's capable hands. I submit my desires and personal agenda to His perfect will for my life. As I talk with Him about the day ahead, He gives me clarity of mind that helps me discern what most needs to get done. The more I learn about what needs to be discarded from my mind and my life, the more room I'll have for my Savior to fill with His joy and peace.

DIANNE NEAL MATTHEWS

FAITH STEP

Each time you notice a negative emotion invade your mind today, stop and tell Jesus one way that He sparks joy in your life.

WEDNESDAY
NOVEMBER 19

As for you, the anointing [the special gift, the preparation] which you received from Him remains [permanently] in you, and you have no need for anyone to teach you. But just as His anointing teaches you [giving you insight through the presence of the Holy Spirit] about all things, and is true and is not a lie, and just as His anointing has taught you, you must remain in Him [being rooted in Him, knit to Him].

1 JOHN 2:27 (AMP)

THIS MORNING I CONDITIONED MY butcher block cutting board.

This sturdy slab of wood sits on my counter all the time. It endures the sharpest of knife cuts. It survives having cheese smeared all over it, tomatoes dripping on it, and onions and garlic scenting it when chopped.

But even the most faithful butcher block needs to be cared for. As I rubbed the special oil into the wood, I felt myself wishing someone would condition me. I've been feeling the knife cuts of life, the scrapes, and the mess. Where can we go to be soothed, healed, and renewed? We can turn to Jesus. We can spend time letting His Word permeate us. He can rub away the marks, scars, and dents, then pour healing oil over our hearts.

The instructions on the wood conditioner say to leave it on for several hours before buffing. Those directions made me smile as I thought about the Word of Jesus. Sometimes I read a quick verse or two and jump up, ready to get on with my day. But my soul needs deep conditioning. I determined to take more time to let the Word sink into my heart, to allow Jesus to anoint me with His truth, wisdom, and healing.

SHARON HINCK

FAITH STEP

Schedule a longer-than-usual time today to sit with Jesus, asking Him to let His Word sink in deeply and bring healing to your soul.

THURSDAY
NOVEMBER 20

He fell on his face at Jesus' feet and thanked him.

LUKE 17:16 (CEB)

SOMETIMES I WONDER HOW PEOPLE without children in their lives learn things. Nieces and nephews, offspring, grandchildren, a Sunday school class, a team to coach, a nursery, babysitting, childcare, adopting, fostering . . . We learn so much by being around children.

Over coffee the other day, young parents told me the story about their two-year-old daughter learning how to pray. They'd videotaped one of her first attempts at praying as she knelt beside her toddler bed. In essence, this is the transcript from her lyrical, little-girl prayer:

"Thank You, Jesus, for my friends. And . . . thank You, Jesus. Jesus, thank You. And . . . Jesus, thank You so much. Thank You soooooo much, Jesus." (Deep breath.) "Jesus, thank You. Thank You, Jesus. Thank You, Jesus, for my friends. Thank You so much. Jesus, thank You. Thank You, Jesus." That wasn't the end. But by this point in the video, the parent holding the camera could hardly stay still. Suppressed laughter shook the camera.

How precious! And how precious it must be for Jesus, on the receiving end of such a prayer. He must have observed that scene and thought, *Finally! Finally someone gets it—how to really pray.*

Simply thanking Him. Nothing fancy. Expressing gratitude in childlike but loving exuberance.

What well-crafted prayer could compare to a sincere heart expressing its gratitude. "Jesus, there's really nothing more to say beyond, 'Thank You.'"

CYNTHIA RUCHTI

FAITH STEP

Spend at least a portion of your prayer time today, if not all of it, saying your heart's version of "Thank You so much, Jesus." Don't be surprised if you hear a whisper from heaven that sounds like divine joy.

FRIDAY
NOVEMBER 21

Jesus was in the stern, sleeping on a cushion. The disciples woke him and said to him, "Teacher, don't you care if we drown?"

MARK 4:38 (NIV)

GENE STUDIED THE WEATHER FORECAST and tide charts for days prior to an overnight sailing trip. We left the dock and motored ninety minutes on the Fraser River until we reached its mouth. That's when wind, tide, and current combined, creating waves bigger than we'd bargained for.

Our boat rocked and heaved. Waves splashed over the stern into the cockpit, where Gene stood at the helm. I sat white-knuckled and wide-eyed. I glanced inside the boat and saw apples and oranges rolling back and forth across the floor. The minifridge's door swung open and spilled eggs, milk, and yogurt onto the rug.

I crawled inside to retrieve the runaway food and positioned myself beside the fridge to hold its door closed.

Nausea hit me within a minute. Suddenly I understood the disciples' fear during storms at sea.

Over time I've pondered their scary sailing trip. Circumstances frightened them, but fear compounded because they doubted Jesus's intent toward them. I understand that thinking. Maybe you do too. Perhaps you've thought, *Jesus, don't You care that we're almost broke? That I'm lonely? That my marriage has ended?*

The truth is, Jesus cares deeply for us just as He cared for His disciples. He knew the storm was coming their way, so He climbed into their boat in advance (Mark 4:36). Friends, He's already in our boats too. Sooner or later the winds will rise and the waves will rock us, but let's remember that He's with us. His intent is not that we panic but that we experience His power and His peace.

GRACE FOX

FAITH STEP

Complete this sentence, filling in the blank with whatever concerns you at this time: I choose to believe that Jesus cares about _____.

SATURDAY
NOVEMBER 22

*But if we hope for what we do not yet have,
we wait for it patiently.*

ROMANS 8:25 (NIV)

BEN, MY FRIEND'S YOUNG SON, suited up in his football gear—helmet, pads, and all—then informed his mom that he was going out to play. After a few minutes, she looked out the window and saw him standing in the backyard alone. Feeling sorry for her little boy, Jana went outside. "Do you want to play something else?" she asked. Ben turned and grinned from within his helmet. "Nope, I'm playing football." Confused, Jana asked, "You are?" Ben nodded the bulky helmet. "Yep, I'm offense. The defense is on the field now."

Jana couldn't see the game Ben visualized, the one obviously still entertaining him while he waited for his turn. But Ben knew that part of playing football involved waiting patiently on the sidelines. He also had the ability to hope for what he didn't yet have, a chance to play.

Often we are the little boy on the sidelines wanting a chance to play. We want to shine for Christ. We want to be needed, have purpose. However, every now and then we need that reminder that contentment may also be found in letting someone else have their time on the field. We should try to be like Ben, quite happy waiting his turn.

RENEE ANDREWS

FAITH STEP

Remember what Christ said in Luke 14:10 and find Ben's joy in waiting your turn.

SUNDAY
NOVEMBER 23

"I, Jesus . . . am . . . the bright Morning Star."

REVELATION 22:16 (NIV)

As I type, the pitch dark outside is giving way to the sunrise. A medium-blue sky peeks over the neighbors' trees while I see next to me the outline of a sweet little girl sleeping in the dark.

Last night our family split up for separate adventures. The guys went to deer camp for Paxton's first hunt this morning, and my daughter and I pulled out the sofa bed for a movie night and slumber party in the family room. Fighting a cold, and unaccustomed to sleeping on the thin mattress, I awoke early and am enjoying the peaceful morning hush.

I love this kind of wake-up. It feels as if I'm sitting here waiting for Jesus to fill me with His heart for the day. There's something special about the morning, something spiritual.

It's easy to take for granted that the morning is just like any other time of day, but Jesus's Word speaks of gifts that come with the morning. When we wake up, He has new mercies to shed on us (Lamentations 3:22–23). The morning scatters the threats of darkness (Luke 1:78–79) and awakens us to His glory (Psalm 57:8). He even calls Himself the bright Morning Star.

The Creator did not have to form our solar system to rotate and revolve so we could experience refreshment and a new beginning every twenty-four hours. But He did. Could it be that His plan and provision for each new day was precisely so that we could be reminded of His care and hope and light so frequently? We need morning eyes to notice Him though.

The sky is light now. A new day has begun, filled with hope, soul care, and awareness of His love if I'm attuned to see Him in it.

Good morning to you.

ERIN KEELEY MARSHALL

FAITH STEP

No matter the hour, ask Jesus to help you see Him today.

MONDAY
NOVEMBER 24

We are God's handiwork, created in Christ Jesus to do good works, which God prepared in advance for us to do.

EPHESIANS 2:10 (NIV)

AFTER A LONG SEASON OF various struggles, I was spending a rare quiet morning in prayer. I was interrupted by the sound of a snare drum in the park across the street. I peered out the window and saw a few high school students gathering. Cars pulled up, and more drummers emerged. Soon an entire drum corps began an amazing rehearsal. And then—even better—they marched down the sidewalk and all the way around our block.

Neighbors emerged and applauded. My spirits lifted at the drummers' musical skills and impressive coordination as they twirled drumsticks and marched in step. Their strong rhythms stirred courage in my heart, as if in answer to my earlier prayers. While I waited for them to come back around, I chatted with my next-door neighbor, whom I hadn't seen in many weeks.

Those students lightened the load of everyone on our block. Celebrating them together brought fellowship to neighbors. A gift of art—whether music, theater, dance, ceramics, fabrics, culinary, painting—has the ability to bring change. No wonder we followers of Jesus are compared to works of art. As we serve Him, we become a vehicle for Him to lift hearts and create unity. Our daily lives can do what that drum corps did for my neighborhood.

I sometimes feel as if I'm an out-of-step drummer who keeps missing the beat. Yet I can trust that, in Jesus, I am His handiwork who will unfold His good works.

SHARON HINCK

FAITH STEP

As a reminder that you are a work of art, create something to share with a friend today in whatever art form you enjoy most.

TUESDAY
NOVEMBER 25

Then Jesus said, "Let's go off by ourselves to a quiet place and rest awhile."

MARK 6:31 (NLT)

YEARS AGO, MY HUSBAND HAD a job assignment in northern Minnesota. When I flew out to see him, we decided to visit a nearby wolf sanctuary. Richard had a phone call on the way, so he pulled off the tree-lined highway and stepped out of the car to get a better signal. I got out to stretch my legs and strolled toward a separate stand of trees up a slight incline. Just ahead I spotted a small clearing, lit by slanting rays of sunlight. It drew me like a magnet, and soon I found myself standing in an open space surrounded by tall trees. I stood, looking up as though mesmerized, vaguely aware of the muffled sounds of cars passing down the highway—yet at the same time enveloped in the quietness of the woods.

I've never forgotten that moment that seemed almost magical. It reminds me of how God has designed us with a built-in need to commune with Him. We live in a noisy, hectic world. Even Jesus needed time away for rest and renewal. It isn't always easy to find that "quiet place," especially for parents. Even if we live alone, it can be hard to get away from the noisiness and chaos in our mind.

I find it easy to connect with God through His creation, but right now, I live in a city subdivision. So I have created a quiet place in my home for my prayer time. I sit in a certain spot with my Bible, journal, and favorite pen. Nearby is a scented candle that I find soothing. These are "spiritual magnets" that draw me in to a place where I can find rest in Jesus.

DIANNE NEAL MATTHEWS

FAITH STEP

If you don't have a consistent routine for quiet time, ask Jesus to help you prepare a special place with spiritual magnets of your own.

WEDNESDAY
NOVEMBER 26

Carry each other's burdens, and in this way you will fulfill the law of Christ.

GALATIANS 6:2 (NIV)

Tears filled my eyes when my husband, Kevin—who's also my pastor—asked me to speak at last year's Thanksgiving service. "Can you speak about why you're thankful for our family?"

"But, honey, our family isn't doing so well."

In the four years since our daughter's divorce, she'd struggled to make ends meet while raising three kids. Our grown son had wrestled with depression for more than twenty years. My ninety-two-year-old widowed mom was quickly declining. What could I offer to encourage others?

Kevin reassured me that while our family isn't perfect, we always support each other. That's what keeps us going. My mind filled with thoughts of the many times we'd helped each other navigate some rough patches. "Well, when you put it that way . . . OK, I'll do it."

I began my remarks by confessing how reluctant I'd been to talk about our messy family, but that Kevin's insight helped me see our situation in a new light. Moist eyes, smiles, and nodding heads responded to my admission about our imperfect family. I said, "Flawlessness isn't what Jesus looks for in a family but rather kindness and encouragement. His example of unconditional love empowers us to stand with each other during the tough times and say, 'I've got your back. I'll walk through this darkness with you.'"

Kevin told me afterward how silent the sanctuary was while I spoke. I was glad I'd listened to him. Our family will never be perfect—whose is? But Jesus has filled us with love for each other that knits our hearts together, a perfect reason to thank Him.

JEANETTE LEVELLIE

FAITH STEP

Think of the ways you can show your gratitude for your imperfect family, from praying for them to cooking their favorite meal to sending a card that says, "I'm glad we're related."

THANKSGIVING DAY
THURSDAY
NOVEMBER 27

"Jesus is 'the stone you builders rejected, which has become the cornerstone.' Salvation is found in no one else, for there is no other name under heaven given to mankind by which we must be saved."

ACTS 4:11–12 (NIV)

AT THANKSGIVING, WE GATHERED FRIENDS and neighbors around an abundant table. The holiday provided a lot of bonding time with my kids, especially with my teenage son, because I put him in charge of decorating the table. He and I had a great time shopping for fabric, cheap glasses to use as vases, river rocks from the craft store. We gathered curly willow branches and fresh sage sprigs from the backyard, mini pumpkins from the farm stand. My son went to work painting branches and pumpkins, arranging them precisely. His artistic talents dovetail with our family mission of hospitality.

We used river rocks as place cards, with each person's name written on their rock. After dinner, we instructed each person to take their rock, and write on its smooth surface what they felt thankful for this Thanksgiving. Then we went around the table and shared our thoughts.

We piled up the rocks, to create a sort of altar. I shared the story from 1 Samuel, when Samuel builds an altar and names it Ebenezer, which means "stone of help," to commemorate how God had answered prayer and helped Israel in a key battle. (See 1 Samuel 7.)

Jesus is our rock. Jesus is our Ebenezer, our stone of help. He is the cornerstone, the very foundation of our faith, on which we can lean and trust. When we take a few moments to remember specific ways that He has helped us thus far, we build a little altar in our hearts. When faith wavers, we can look at the altar and be assured that He will help us again.

KERI WYATT KENT

FAITH STEP

Take a smooth stone and a permanent marker, and write a reminder of Jesus's help on it. Put it somewhere you can see it each day.

FRIDAY
NOVEMBER 28

I will make every effort to see that after my departure you will always be able to remember these things.

2 PETER 1:15 (NIV)

THERE WAS A FESTIVE AIR in the small room filled with wrapping paper, ribbon, bows, and countless bags stuffed with gifts. Lively gospel music played in the background as five of us chattered away while we busily wrapped toys, clothing, and games to give away to families for my church's massive community holiday outreach.

I had decided to volunteer on this particular November afternoon to honor my father, who had passed away exactly a year ago on Thanksgiving Day. Dad loved to bless others, so there was no better way for me to spend the first anniversary of his Homegoing than by volunteering for this project.

Dad set an example of giving his time and talents to the church and its people. He loved the Lord and taught his children to do the same. My father delighted in spending time with his family, and we often heard him say, "Precious memories," whenever he recalled an occasion like Thanksgiving that made him smile. He wanted us to also remember those good times—and we do, even though he is no longer physically with us.

Peter told the first-century Christians that he, too, wanted them to remember all that he had taught them—his words of encouragement as well as his admonishments—especially the truths about Jesus. He also wanted them to stand firm in their faith. My dad, like Peter, desired the same for those he loved. And for that I will be eternally thankful.

BARBRANDA LUMPKINS WALLS

FAITH STEP

Write down special memories and truths about Jesus for which you are thankful. Include them in your prayers.

SATURDAY
NOVEMBER 29

And he said to them, "Take care, and be on your guard against all covetousness, for one's life does not consist in the abundance of his possessions."

LUKE 12:15 (ESV)

MINIMALISM HAS BEEN A POPULAR topic in recent years. Adventurous folk are moving into tiny houses. Others are tidying their belongings with fervor. Many fight to stem the tide of materialism in their lives.

Throughout our married life, my hubby and I made an effort to keep our possessions under control. This was challenging when grandparents showered our children with gifts, or coupons from the local craft store tempted me to stock up on supplies each week. A tight budget didn't make a difference. We still managed to accumulate clothes and books from yard sales and thrift stores.

This past year, Ted and I dove into sorting and simplifying. My husband admits he is a "better keep it just in case" guy. He isn't the only one. As we emptied closets, I was amazed at how many things I had carried with me through the years—and forgotten about. We set a goal to get rid of about a quarter of everything. Each decision challenged us to trust that if we ever again needed the "just in case" items, Jesus would provide. We weren't using many of the items we owned, but they brought us a sense of security. However, we've found great joy in letting things go and a new gratitude for all He has granted, and we've determined to be better stewards of those items that remain.

The words of Jesus in Luke aren't a call to deprivation and suffering but are a joyful invitation to focus on what really matters in life: loving Him and loving others.

SHARON HINCK

FAITH STEP

Rummage in the back of a closet or cupboard. Choose items to give away, praying they will bless others.

SUNDAY
NOVEMBER 30

"The Lord your God will be with you wherever you go."

JOSHUA 1:9 (NIV)

My friend and I had been invited to a reading event two hours from our homes. My friend came from the southern part of the state, and I drove from the west.

The setting was everything you'd want in a reading event. A charming coffee shop with warm lighting, a stone fireplace, hardwood floors, good food, and great ambience. Holding a microphone and reading to the crowd gathered for that purpose stirred no uneasiness and no fear. It was a comfortable setting with attentive listeners.

The discomfort came later. We'd left one of our cars at the hotel where we'd stay the night. After the event, we assumed we'd find our way back with little trouble. But unfamiliar surroundings and my phone's slow-to-respond navigation system meant "I think it's this way" turned out to be "It's not this way."

Getting lost made us panic briefly. But after a few moments of unease, we switched to having a sense of adventure. Why? Because we remembered that Jesus has our back in every situation—large or small. He goes before us, behind us, and beside us. All need for fear evaporates when He's the backseat driver (or when He "takes the wheel").

Our unexpected route took us along a beautiful lake, just as the sun was saying its brilliant, colorful goodbyes for the day. Longer and slower, the backroad was just what our souls needed.

Sometimes Jesus gives us courage by standing between us and danger. Sometimes it's His still small voice from the backseat saying, "It'll be OK. Let's have an adventure."

CYNTHIA RUCHTI

FAITH STEP

Take an unexpected route today. Note the wonders you may have missed if you hadn't detoured. Thank Jesus for accompanying you wherever you go.

Autumn and Thanksgiving 2025
Reflections and Memories

Autumn and Thanksgiving 2025
Reflections and Memories

Autumn and Thanksgiving 2025
Reflections and Memories

Autumn and Thanksgiving 2025
Reflections and Memories

Contributors

Renee Andrews 82, 112

Rebecca Barlow Jordan 10, 56, 76, 94

Jeannie Blackmer 48

Pat Butler Dyson 18, 60

Suzanne Davenport Tietjen 28

Gwen Ford Faulkenberry 8, 64, 100

Susanna Foth Aughtmon 14, 22, 34, 52, 66, 78

Grace Fox 26, 42, 62, 98, 110

Heidi Gaul 6, 32, 50, 86, 96

Sharon Hinck 20, 40, 74, 88, 106, 116, 126

Erin Keeley Marshall 36, 46, 58, 114

Jeanette Levellie 120

Barbranda Lumpkins Walls 124

Dianne Neal Matthews 16, 38, 80, 104, 118

Cynthia Ruchti 12, 44, 72, 84, 90, 108, 128

Camy Tang 30, 92

Cassandra Tiersma 54, 70

Keri Wyatt Kent 24, 102, 122

Acknowledgements

Scripture quotations marked (AMP) are taken from the *Amplified Bible*. Copyright © 2015 by The Lockman Foundation, La Habra, California. All rights reserved.

Scripture quotations marked (CEB) are taken from the *Common English Bible*. Copyright © 2011 by Common English Bible.

Scripture quotations marked (ESV) are taken from *The Holy Bible, English Standard Version*. Copyright © 2001 by Crossway Bibles, a division of Good News Publishers. Used by permission. All rights reserved.

Scripture quotations marked (GW) are taken from *GOD'S WORD*®. Copyright © 1995, 2003, 2013, 2014, 2019, 2020 by God's Word to the Nations Mission Society. Used by permission.

Scripture quotations marked (HCSB) are taken from the *Holman Christian Standard Bible*. Copyright © 1999, 2000, 2002, 2003, 2009 by Holman Bible Publishers, Nashville, Tennessee. All rights reserved.

Scripture quotations marked (KJV) are taken from the *King James Version of the Bible*.

Scripture quotations marked (NCV) are taken from *The Holy Bible, New Century Version*. Copyright © 2005 by Thomas Nelson.

Scripture quotations marked (NIV) are taken from *The Holy Bible, New International Version*®, *NIV*®. Copyright © 1973, 1978, 1984, 2011 by Biblica, Inc. Used by permission. All rights reserved worldwide.

Scripture quotations marked (NKJV) are taken from the *New King James Version*®. Copyright © 1982 by Thomas Nelson. Used by permission. All rights reserved.

Scripture quotations marked (NLT) are taken from the *Holy Bible, New Living Translation*. Copyright © 1996, 2004, 2007, 2015 by Tyndale House Foundation. Used by permission of Tyndale House Publishers Inc., Carol Stream, Illinois. All rights reserved.

Scripture quotations marked (TLB) are taken from *The Living Bible*. Copyright © 1971 by Tyndale House Publishers, Inc., Carol Stream, Illinois. All rights reserved.

A Note from the Editors

We hope you enjoyed *Walking with Jesus: Devotions for Autumn & Thanksgiving 2025*, published by Guideposts. For more than 75 years, Guideposts, a nonprofit organization, has been driven by a vision of a world filled with hope. We aspire to be the voice of a trusted friend, a friend who makes you feel more hopeful and connected.

By making a purchase from Guideposts, you join our community in touching millions of lives, inspiring them to believe that all things are possible through faith, hope, and prayer. Your continued support allows us to provide uplifting resources to those in need. Whether through our communities, websites, apps, or publications, we inspire our audiences, bring them together, and comfort, uplift, entertain, and guide them. Visit us at guideposts.org to learn more.

We would love to hear from you. Write us at Guideposts, P.O. Box 5815, Harlan, Iowa 51593, or call us at (800) 932-2145. Did you love *Walking with Jesus: Devotions for Autumn & Thanksgiving 2025*? Leave a review for this product on guideposts.org/shop. Your feedback helps others in our community find relevant products.

Find inspiration, find faith, find Guideposts.

Shop our best sellers and favorites at
guideposts.org/shop

Or scan the QR code to go directly to our Shop